Martial Law and Political Turmoil: The Yoon Suk Yeol Saga

A Nation's Reckoning: Unraveling the Constitutional Crisis, Impeachment Drama and the Fight for Democracy in South Korea

Victor L. Wilson

Copyright © Victor L. Wilson

2024

All rights reserved, No part of this publication may be reproduced, distributed, or transmitted in any form or by any means, including photocopying, recording, or other electronic or mechanical methods, without the prior written permission of the publisher, except in the case of brief quotations embodied in critical reviews and certain other noncommercial uses permitted by copyright law.

Table Of Contents

Introduction
Significance of the Recent Events in South Korea

Chapter One; Historical Context of Martial Law in South Korea
Legacy of Military Rule
Previous Instances of Martial Law
Transition to Democracy in the Late 1980s

Chapter Two; The Political Landscape
President Yoon Suk Yeol: Background and Rise to Power
The Role of Opposition Parties
Current Political Tensions and Public Sentiment

Chapter Three; The Declaration of Martial Law
Circumstances Leading to the Declaration

Yoon's Justifications: Threats and Accusations
Immediate Reactions from Political Factions

Chapter Four; Implementation of Martial Law
Powers Granted Under Martial Law
Restrictions Imposed: Civil Liberties and Freedoms
Role of Military Commanders and Enforcement Actions

Chapter Five; Public Response and Civil Society
Protests Against Martial Law
Media Coverage and Public Discourse
Voices from Civil Society: Activists and Citizens

Chapter Six; The Lifting of Martial Law
Parliamentary Actions Against Martial Law

President Yoon's Decision to Rescind the Declaration
Implications of the Lifting for Governance

Chapter Seven; Impeachment Proceedings
Grounds for Impeachment: Legal Framework
Political Maneuvering and Party Dynamics
The Vote and Immediate Consequences

Chapter Eight; Comparative Analysis
Martial Law in Other Democracies
Lessons Learned from Historical Precedents
The Role of International Relations in Martial Law Declarations
The Global Impact of Martial Law

Chapter Nine; Future Implications for South Korea
Political Stability and Governance Challenges
The Role of International Relations, Especially with North Korea
Prospects for Democratic Resilience

Conclusion

Introduction

This book delves into one of South Korea's most turbulent political episodes—the declaration of martial law by President Yoon Suk Yeol on December 3, 2024. Designed as a detailed examination of the unfolding crisis, the book seeks to capture not just the events themselves but their underlying causes, implications, and the emotional impact on South Korea's citizens.

The purpose here is twofold: first, to document the sequence of events for a global audience seeking clarity in a time of confusion; second, to explore the broader themes of democracy, political accountability, and governance under stress. Through a factual yet human-centered approach, this book aims to connect readers with the real-life consequences of political turmoil. In every chapter, you'll find voices from across the political and social spectrum—politicians battling over constitutional interpretations, citizens protesting on the streets, and experts analyzing the fragile dynamics of leadership. This book is not just a historical record; it's a reflection on the fragility and resilience of democracy itself.

Significance of the Recent Events in South Korea

The events surrounding President Yoon Suk Yeol's martial law declaration represent a watershed moment in South Korea's political history. For a nation that transitioned to democracy only in the late 1980s after decades of authoritarian rule, the specter of martial law rekindles painful memories and hard-won lessons.

President Yoon's decision to invoke military control over civilian life sent shockwaves across South Korea and beyond. His justification—that the opposition-dominated parliament was colluding with North Korea to undermine governance—was as audacious as it was polarizing. For his critics, it smacked of desperation and overreach; for his supporters, it was a bold move to safeguard national security. Within hours of the declaration, the National Assembly voted to nullify martial law, a dramatic countermeasure that underscored the depth of South Korea's political polarization. The tension in Seoul was palpable: in one neighborhood, young activists organized peaceful marches, their placards decrying "tyranny in disguise." Across the city, citizens who remembered the brutal days of past regimes voiced their anger, fear, and disbelief.

These events are more than a political crisis; they are a test of South Korea's democratic institutions and the will of its people. President Yoon's declining approval ratings, coupled with a series of scandals involving his administration, had already put his leadership under scrutiny. The martial law declaration amplified calls for his resignation and opened the door for impeachment proceedings that could fundamentally alter the country's leadership.

But the story doesn't stop there. Beyond the headlines, this crisis touches on larger themes: the role of civil society in challenging authority, the checks and balances inherent in a democracy, and the responsibility of leaders to uphold the principles they swore to defend. It also brings into sharp focus South Korea's geopolitical challenges, particularly its fraught relationship with North Korea and its reliance on international alliances. For citizens, this crisis isn't merely a political drama; it's deeply personal. From university campuses to corporate offices, debates rage about the implications of these events. What does it mean to live in a democracy if the very institutions meant to protect it are at risk of manipulation? How does a society heal from such deep divisions, and what can ordinary people do to safeguard their freedoms?

This book captures those questions and more. Through detailed analysis and emotional storytelling, it provides a window into South Korea's present turmoil while offering insights into the universal struggles of governance, power, and democracy.

As you turn the pages, you will encounter not just facts and figures but the lived experiences of those caught in the storm of history. This is a story about politics, yes, but also about resilience, courage, and the enduring fight for a better tomorrow. With the benefit of hindsight and the clarity of thoughtful investigation, this book seeks to bring light to the chaos, offering readers a comprehensive understanding of a moment that will be studied for decades to come.

Chapter One; Historical Context of Martial Law in South Korea

Legacy of Military Rule

To understand the gravity of President Yoon Suk Yeol's 2024 martial law declaration, one must look back at South Korea's tumultuous history with military rule. South Korea's journey from authoritarianism to democracy was neither smooth nor inevitable. For decades, the country was gripped by strongman leaders who wielded power with an iron fist, often under the guise of maintaining order and security.

After the Korean War (1950–1953), South Korea faced political and economic instability. It was during this fragile period that military leaders began to dominate the political landscape. Park Chung-hee, a former general, seized power in 1961 through a coup. His rule, while marked by economic transformation, was characterized by political repression and the suspension of democratic freedoms. Martial law became a tool for silencing dissent and consolidating control.

The most infamous episode of martial law in South Korea occurred in 1980. Following the assassination of Park Chung-hee in 1979, General Chun Doo-hwan orchestrated another coup and imposed martial law across the nation. This led to the Gwangju Uprising, where citizens protesting for democracy were met with brutal military force, resulting in the deaths of hundreds. The scars of this event linger in South Korea's collective memory, serving as a stark reminder of the dangers of unchecked power.

The legacy of military rule has left an indelible mark on South Korea's psyche. While the country has since transitioned to a vibrant democracy, the fear of returning to authoritarian practices remains ever-present. This historical backdrop is essential to understanding why Yoon's 2024 declaration of martial law triggered such a visceral reaction from the public and political leaders alike.

Previous Instances of Martial Law

Before the late 1980s, martial law was a recurring feature in South Korea's governance. From the Korean War to the political crises of the 1960s and 1970s, successive leaders invoked martial law to quell unrest, citing threats to national security or political stability.

In 1948, during the aftermath of the Jeju Uprising, martial law was declared to suppress what the government called communist insurgents. Tens of thousands of civilians were killed or displaced in what is now recognized as one of the darkest chapters of modern Korean history. This early use of martial law set a precedent for its deployment as a means of suppressing dissent, rather than addressing genuine threats. The 1980 martial law under Chun Doo-hwan, however, became a turning point. The brutality of the military crackdown in Gwangju galvanized opposition to authoritarian rule and planted the seeds for South Korea's pro-democracy movement. By the time martial law was lifted later that year, the demand for democratic reforms had become unstoppable, leading to the eventual democratic transition in 1987.

These historical instances underscore how martial law has often been a double-edged sword. While leaders used it to assert control, it also fueled resistance and paved the way for transformative change. The events of 2024 are now poised to follow this historical pattern, raising questions about the future of South Korean democracy.

Transition to Democracy in the Late 1980s

The late 1980s marked a watershed moment in South Korea's history. After years of struggle, the country finally broke free from the grip of military dictatorships. The June Democratic Uprising of 1987 was the culmination of years of public discontent, sparked by the authoritarian excesses of the Chun Doo-hwan regime and the assassination of pro-democracy activist Park Jong-chul.

The streets of Seoul and other major cities became battlegrounds for citizens demanding change. University students, labor unions, and ordinary citizens rallied together, united by their desire for a democratic future. Their efforts paid off when Chun's government conceded to the people's demands, paving the way for direct presidential elections and significant constitutional reforms.

South Korea's transition to democracy was nothing short of remarkable. In just a few years, it transformed from a military dictatorship into a robust democracy with free elections, an independent judiciary, and a vibrant civil society. This period also saw the establishment of safeguards designed to prevent the misuse of martial law, reflecting the lessons learned from decades of abuse.

However, as the events of 2024 demonstrate, even the most resilient democracies are not immune to challenges. The declaration of martial law by President Yoon has reignited debates about the balance of power, the role of the military in governance, and the fragility of democratic institutions. For many South Koreans, the return of martial law in 2024 felt like a betrayal of the democratic ideals that so many had fought and died to achieve. "We thought those days were behind us," said one elderly protester in Seoul, holding a faded photograph of herself marching in the 1987 rallies. "To see it happen again—it's like a nightmare we can't escape."

The younger generation, born in the post-dictatorship era, responded with equal fervor. Social media platforms were flooded with messages condemning the declaration, with hashtags like #NeverAgain trending globally. Activists organized candlelight vigils reminiscent of the protests that had ousted President Park Geun-hye in 2017, signaling that the spirit of resistance remains strong.

But the declaration also exposed deep divisions within South Korean society. While many viewed it as a dangerous overreach, others supported Yoon's actions, believing his claims that the opposition was colluding with North Korea. This divide mirrors the political polarization that has come to define South Korea in recent years, making it clear that the country's democratic journey is far from over. This chapter sets the stage for understanding the events of 2024 in their proper historical context. By examining South Korea's past struggles with martial law and it's hard-fought transition to democracy, readers can better appreciate the stakes involved in the current crisis.

The next chapter will delve into the political landscape leading up to Yoon's controversial decision, offering insights into the personalities, parties, and policies that shaped this pivotal moment.

Chapter Two; The Political Landscape

President Yoon Suk Yeol: Background and Rise to Power

President Yoon Suk Yeol's political journey has been anything but conventional. A career prosecutor known for his relentless pursuit of justice, Yoon first gained national recognition for his role in high-profile corruption cases. His no-nonsense approach to tackling graft, even at the highest levels of government, earned him both admiration and enemies.

Yoon's ascent to the presidency in 2022 was a testament to his appeal as an outsider willing to challenge the status quo. Campaigning on a platform of transparency, reform, and economic revitalization, he struck a chord with voters weary of political scandals and stagnation. Yet, his tenure has been anything but smooth.

From the outset, Yoon's administration faced significant hurdles, including economic uncertainty, tensions with North Korea, and growing political polarization. His hardline stance on national security and willingness to confront opposition lawmakers head-on earned him a reputation as a divisive leader. While his supporters praised his boldness, critics accused him of authoritarian tendencies and a lack of willingness to build consensus.

By 2024, Yoon's approval ratings had taken a nosedive. A series of scandals involving close associates, combined with perceived mismanagement of domestic and foreign policy, fueled public dissatisfaction. His declaration of martial law amid mounting political tension seemed, to many, like the culmination of a presidency teetering on the edge of crisis.

The Role of Opposition Parties

South Korea's political landscape has long been characterized by fierce rivalry between its major parties, and the current crisis is no exception. The Democratic Party of Korea (DPK), which holds a majority in the National Assembly, has been a formidable opponent to Yoon's conservative People Power Party (PPP).

The DPRK's dominance in parliament has allowed it to challenge Yoon's policies at every turn, creating a climate of legislative gridlock. Accusations of obstructionism have flown in both directions, with Yoon's administration accusing the DPK of sabotaging governance, while the opposition contends that it is merely holding the president accountable.

The lead-up to the martial law declaration was marked by escalating tensions. Opposition lawmakers accused Yoon of attempting to undermine democratic norms, citing his combative rhetoric and refusal to engage in dialogue. For their part, the DPK positioned itself as the defender of democracy, rallying public support against what it portrayed as Yoon's authoritarian overreach. This rivalry reached its zenith on December 3, 2024, when the National Assembly swiftly nullified Yoon's martial law declaration. The speed and decisiveness of their response highlighted the opposition's unity and determination to prevent a return to autocracy. Yet, it also underscored the deep divisions within South Korean politics, where compromise often takes a back seat to confrontation.

Current Political Tensions and Public Sentiment

South Korea's political climate in 2024 is a reflection of broader societal trends. Economic inequality, generational divides, and regional rivalries have all contributed to a sense of disillusionment with traditional politics. These underlying issues have made the public more receptive to populist rhetoric and less trusting of political institutions.

Yoon's presidency has been both a symptom and a cause of this polarization. His supporters, many of whom are older and conservative, view him as a necessary counterbalance to what they perceive as the excesses of progressive politics. They believe his tough stance on North Korea and emphasis on national security are essential in a time of global uncertainty. On the other side, younger, more progressive South Koreans see Yoon as out of touch with modern values. His policies on social issues, including gender equality and labor rights, have drawn criticism from activists and younger voters. For this demographic, Yoon's martial law declaration was not just a political misstep but a betrayal of the democratic principles they hold dear.

Public protests in the aftermath of the declaration revealed the depth of this divide. While tens of thousands took to the streets to demand Yoon's resignation, smaller counter-protests voiced support for his actions, citing the need to maintain order and address perceived threats from North Korea. The stark contrast between these groups highlights the challenges of governing a nation increasingly split along ideological lines.

Amid the political wrangling and public demonstrations, it is easy to lose sight of the human stories at the heart of this crisis. For many South Koreans, the events of December 2024 have sparked feelings of anger, fear, and uncertainty. "It feels like we're back in the 1980s," said a university professor who participated in the protests against Yoon's martial law declaration. "We fought so hard for democracy, and now it feels like all of that is slipping away." For others, the crisis has reinforced the importance of vigilance in protecting democratic freedoms. "This is a wake-up call," said a young activist. "We can't take democracy for granted. It's something we have to fight for every day."

These sentiments reflect a broader reckoning within South Korea, as citizens grapple with the fragility of their political system and the role they must play in safeguarding it. Whether through protests, public discourse, or voting, the people of South Korea are making their voices heard in ways that will shape the country's future.

The political landscape leading up to President Yoon Suk Yeol's martial law declaration is one of intense division and competing visions for South Korea's future. At the heart of the crisis lies a battle over the soul of the nation: a struggle between authoritarian impulses and democratic ideals, between fear and hope.

Chapter Three; The Declaration of Martial Law

Circumstances Leading to the Declaration

The lead-up to President Yoon Suk Yeol's martial law declaration on December 3, 2024, was marked by escalating tensions both within and outside the government. The president had been embroiled in an intensifying political battle with the Democratic Party of Korea (DPK), which held a majority in the National Assembly. Accusations of corruption, alleged ties between opposition lawmakers and North Korea, and legislative roadblocks created an atmosphere of distrust and dysfunction.

Yoon's administration was already under immense pressure. Economic stagnation, rising living costs, and scandals involving high-ranking officials had eroded public confidence. Protests and labor strikes were becoming frequent, further straining an already fragile political environment. The president's approval ratings had plummeted to historic lows, leaving his leadership vulnerable.

Against this backdrop, President Yoon accused the opposition of actively undermining his administration and collaborating with foreign adversaries, particularly North Korea. He claimed the National Assembly's actions, including their obstruction of key defense bills, posed an imminent threat to national security. This rhetoric set the stage for what would become the most controversial moment of his presidency.

In a nationally televised address, Yoon declared martial law, citing the need to "restore order and protect the integrity of the state." The announcement granted the military sweeping powers to maintain public order and temporarily curtailed civil liberties, including freedom of assembly and press. For many, this was a shocking escalation that crossed a line few thought would ever be breached in post-democratic South Korea.

Yoon's Justifications: Threats and Accusations

President Yoon's justification for martial law rested on claims of imminent threats from both domestic and foreign sources. In his speech, he outlined what he described as a "conspiracy" between opposition leaders and North Korean agents to destabilize the government.

He alleged that confidential intelligence reports had uncovered a coordinated effort to sow chaos through protests, strikes, and legislative paralysis. These accusations, however, were met with widespread skepticism. Opposition lawmakers, civil society groups, and even members of Yoon's own party questioned the validity of the claims, pointing out that no concrete evidence was provided. Critics argued that the president was using national security as a pretext to consolidate power and silence dissent.

For Yoon's supporters, the justification resonated. They saw his actions as necessary to address a perceived lack of accountability within the opposition and to safeguard the nation against external threats. Some pointed to North Korea's history of covert operations in the South as evidence that such threats should not be taken lightly. The polarizing nature of Yoon's justifications highlighted the deep divisions within South Korean society. While some citizens rallied behind the president's call for unity and vigilance, others viewed it as an alarming echo of the country's authoritarian past.

Immediate Reactions from Political Factions

The declaration of martial law triggered swift and dramatic responses from all corners of South Korea's political spectrum. Within hours, the opposition-controlled National Assembly convened an emergency session to nullify the declaration. Lawmakers denounced the move as unconstitutional and accused Yoon of betraying his oath to uphold democratic principles.

Their efforts culminated in a near-unanimous vote to repeal martial law, a rare display of unity in a chamber often characterized by bitter partisanship. This legislative action set the stage for a direct confrontation between the executive and legislative branches, with both sides claiming to act in the nation's best interest. Outside the Assembly, political parties mobilized their supporters. The Democratic Party of Korea organized nationwide protests, drawing tens of thousands of citizens who demanded Yoon's resignation. Chanting slogans like "Democracy, not dictatorship," these protests reflected the growing anger and fear among the public.

Meanwhile, Yoon's conservative People Power Party (PPP) scrambled to defend the president's actions. Though some party members expressed private concerns about the implications of martial law, the party leadership publicly supported Yoon, framing the declaration as a necessary measure in extraordinary circumstances. This internal tension within the PPP foreshadowed potential fractures in the president's political base.

For ordinary citizens, the immediate aftermath of the martial law declaration was a mix of confusion, fear, and defiance. The sudden curtailment of civil liberties, including restrictions on movement and public gatherings, evoked painful memories of past authoritarian regimes. Many older South Koreans, who had lived through the martial law era of the 1970s and 1980s, described feeling a sense of déjà vu. "I thought we had left this behind," said a 67-year-old retired teacher in Gwangju, the site of the 1980 uprising against military rule. "To see it happening again, it's heartbreaking."

Younger South Koreans, many of whom had grown up in a democratic society, reacted with a mix of outrage and disbelief. Social media became a powerful tool for organizing protests and spreading information, with hashtags like #StopMartialLaw and #SaveOurDemocracy trending globally.

The business community also felt the impact. Markets reacted negatively to the announcement, with stock prices plummeting as investors worried about the implications of political instability. Small business owners, already struggling with economic challenges, expressed concerns about the potential for prolonged unrest and its impact on their livelihoods. In rural areas, where support for Yoon was traditionally stronger, reactions were more subdued. Some residents voiced cautious support for the president, citing concerns about national security and trust in his leadership. Others, however, questioned whether martial law was truly necessary, reflecting a growing sense of unease even among Yoon's core supporters.

The declaration of martial law marked a turning point in South Korea's political crisis. It not only intensified the conflict between the president and the National Assembly but also deepened divisions within society. As the immediate shock subsided, the focus shifted to what would come next: the lifting of martial law and the legal and political battles that would follow.

Chapter Four; Implementation of Martial Law

Powers Granted Under Martial Law

President Yoon Suk Yeol's declaration of martial law represented a profound shift in the balance of power within South Korea. Under this extraordinary measure, the military was granted sweeping authority to oversee public order and enforce national security directives. Civilian law enforcement agencies were effectively sidelined, with military commanders taking charge of operations in urban centers and regions of strategic importance.

The martial law decree enabled the suspension of several constitutional rights, including freedom of assembly, speech, and the press. Censorship was immediately imposed on media outlets deemed critical of the government, while social media platforms faced stringent monitoring to prevent the dissemination of what the administration labeled as "subversive content."

Curfews were enforced nationwide, with citizens required to remain indoors during designated hours unless granted special permits. Public gatherings of more than five people were prohibited, effectively halting protests and labor strikes. These measures were justified by the administration as essential to restoring stability and thwarting potential threats to national security.

The financial sector was not spared from scrutiny. The martial law decree included provisions allowing the government to freeze assets and accounts suspected of funding "anti-state activities." These actions added another layer of fear and uncertainty, as citizens worried about being wrongly accused of subversion.

Restrictions Imposed: Civil Liberties and Freedoms

For many South Koreans, the most immediate impact of martial law was the sudden erosion of personal freedoms. The government's strict enforcement measures created an atmosphere of pervasive fear, with citizens wary of speaking out or even gathering informally.

The press, once a vibrant pillar of South Korea's democracy, became one of the first casualties. Newsrooms were raided, and editors were instructed to remove content critical of the administration. Independent journalists faced harassment, arrests, and even physical intimidation, while state-run media outlets churned out pro-government narratives.

One reporter, who asked to remain anonymous, described the chilling effects of the censorship: "Overnight, we went from being watchdogs of democracy to being muzzled by those in power. It's devastating to see the public's right to know stripped away like this." Educational institutions were also targeted. Universities, traditionally hotbeds of political activism, were placed under surveillance, and several student leaders were detained for alleged anti-government activities. Professors were warned against discussing politically sensitive topics, further stifling intellectual freedom.

The military's presence on the streets was another stark reminder of the authoritarian shift. Armed soldiers patrolled public spaces, conducting random identity checks and dispersing gatherings. For many citizens, the sight of tanks and barricades in city centers was both surreal and terrifying.

Role of Military Commanders and Enforcement Actions

The military played a central role in enforcing martial law, with commanders granted unprecedented authority over civilian affairs. The chain of command bypassed traditional civilian oversight, giving military leaders significant autonomy in implementing the president's directives.

General Kim Ji-hoon, appointed as the de facto head of martial law enforcement, emerged as a controversial figure. Known for his loyalty to President Yoon and his hardline stance on national security, Kim oversaw the deployment of troops to major cities, including Seoul, Busan, and Daegu. His directives emphasized zero tolerance for dissent, resulting in widespread crackdowns on protests and perceived acts of defiance.

One of the most controversial incidents occurred in Seoul, where a peaceful demonstration against martial law was met with an aggressive military response. Tear gas, water cannons, and rubber bullets were used to disperse the crowd, resulting in numerous injuries and arrests. Eyewitness accounts painted a grim picture of the chaos, with one protester describing the scene as "a battlefield in the heart of our capital."

Rural areas experienced a different dynamic. While urban centers faced heavy-handed enforcement, smaller towns saw a more subdued military presence. In some cases, local commanders took a more lenient approach, focusing on maintaining order rather than suppressing dissent. This uneven implementation of martial law highlighted the varying interpretations of Yoon's directives within the military ranks. Amid the sweeping measures and dramatic displays of power, the human cost of martial law became increasingly evident. Stories of individuals caught in the crossfire emerged, shedding light on the personal struggles faced by ordinary citizens.

A 29-year-old office worker in Seoul recounted the fear she felt returning home late from work during the first night of the curfew. "The streets were eerily quiet, and the sight of soldiers on every corner was terrifying. I felt like a criminal just for being outside."

Small business owners, already grappling with economic hardships, found themselves further burdened by the restrictions. A café owner in Busan shared his frustration: "My business is barely surviving, and now I can't even open during curfew hours. It feels like we're being punished for something we didn't do." Families were also affected, particularly those with young children or elderly relatives. A mother in Daegu described how her 10-year-old son asked if they were at war after seeing soldiers outside their apartment building. "How do you explain something like this to a child?" she asked, her voice tinged with despair.

Despite the oppressive environment, acts of quiet resistance began to emerge. Underground networks of activists used encrypted messaging apps to coordinate efforts and share information. Students and civil society groups found creative ways to protest, such as wearing symbolic colors or displaying coded messages in public.

These acts of defiance, while small, demonstrated the resilience of South Korea's democratic spirit. For many, they were a reminder that even in the darkest times, the fight for freedom and justice continues. The implementation of martial law under President Yoon Suk Yeol marked one of the most tumultuous periods in South Korea's modern history. The restrictions on civil liberties, the pervasive military presence, and the heavy-handed enforcement measures left an indelible mark on the nation. While the government framed these actions as necessary for national security, the human cost and societal impact raised profound questions about the balance between order and freedom.

Chapter Five; Public Response and Civil Society

Protests Against Martial Law

The public response to President Yoon Suk Yeol's declaration of martial law was immediate and overwhelming. Within hours of the announcement, South Koreans from all walks of life began mobilizing to voice their opposition. The streets of major cities, including Seoul and Gwangju, filled with protesters carrying signs that read, "Democracy, Not Dictatorship," and "End Martial Law Now."

The protests quickly grew in size and intensity, despite the government's ban on public gatherings. Crowds of students, workers, and families defied curfews and risked arrest to march for their rights. In Seoul's Gwanghwamun Square, tens of thousands gathered in what became the largest demonstration since the pro-democracy movement of the 1980s.

While the protests were largely peaceful, the military's response was swift and forceful. Troops used tear gas, water cannons, and rubber bullets to disperse crowds. Videos of confrontations between protesters and armed soldiers went viral, sparking outrage both domestically and internationally. A particularly striking image of a young student holding a sign in front of a row of armed soldiers became a symbol of resistance, echoing iconic moments from past struggles for democracy.

Despite the risks, the protesters remained steadfast. Many drew inspiration from South Korea's history of resistance to authoritarianism. "Our parents fought for democracy," said a university student in Busan. "It's our turn to protect it."

Media Coverage and Public Discourse

The role of the media in shaping public opinion during the martial law crisis was both vital and precarious. Independent journalists and media outlets faced significant challenges under the government's censorship policies, but they worked tirelessly to report the truth.

Some journalists took great personal risks to document the events unfolding on the ground. Videos of protests, interviews with citizens, and exposés on the government's actions were shared through underground networks and social media platforms, bypassing official channels. These efforts ensured that the public had access to uncensored information, fueling the growing resistance.

Social media became a battleground for truth and propaganda. While the government attempted to control the narrative by promoting pro-martial law messaging, citizens used platforms like Twitter and Instagram to share real-time updates and organize protests. Hashtags such as #StopMartialLaw and #DefendDemocracy trended globally, drawing attention to the crisis from international audiences. However, the information war also brought challenges. The spread of misinformation and fear mongering created confusion and panic among citizens. Rumors of mass arrests and military crackdowns circulated widely, leading some to question the reliability of the information they were receiving.

Despite these hurdles, the power of collective voices online and offline proved formidable. Public discourse became a rallying point for South Koreans determined to hold their leaders accountable. Citizens' forums, both virtual and in-person, discussed the implications of martial law and strategized ways to resist it.

Voices from Civil Society: Activists and Citizens

Civil society organizations played a crucial role in amplifying the voices of those most affected by martial law. Activist groups, human rights organizations, and labor unions worked tirelessly to document abuses and support those targeted by the government's heavy-handed measures.

Human rights lawyers provided pro bono services to detained protesters, ensuring that they had legal representation. Religious leaders, including pastors, monks, and priests, opened their places of worship as sanctuaries for activists. In one notable instance, a church in Seoul became a safe haven for students escaping military patrols, with the congregation providing food and shelter.

Ordinary citizens also found ways to resist. A mother in Daegu organized a neighborhood group to distribute pamphlets explaining the legal and constitutional implications of martial law. A small business owner in Incheon provided free meals to protesters, saying, "This is my way of contributing to the fight for our democracy."

The bravery of individuals stood out in stark contrast to the climate of fear imposed by the government. Among these voices was Ji-young, a nurse from Gwangju who became an accidental symbol of the movement. She was photographed standing between a line of soldiers and injured protesters, her white uniform stained with blood. "I'm just doing my job," she said later. "Helping people, no matter which side they're on." These acts of courage and solidarity inspired others to join the movement. Civil society's resilience underscored the deep-seated commitment of South Koreans to protect their democratic values. The martial law crisis took a profound emotional toll on the nation. Families were torn apart as some members supported the government's actions while others protested against them. The strain of living under constant surveillance and the fear of arrest left many feeling anxious and powerless.

"I can't sleep at night," admitted a teacher in Jeonju. "I worry about my students who are out there protesting, and I worry about what kind of future we're leaving for them."

Despite these challenges, hope remained a driving force. Communities came together in acts of collective care, from organizing food drives for protesters to offering free childcare for parents attending demonstrations. The sense of unity fostered a belief that, even in the darkest times, South Korea's democratic spirit would endure. The public response to martial law was a testament to the resilience of South Korea's democratic ideals. From the courage of protesters in the streets to the determination of journalists and activists, the collective efforts of civil society revealed a nation unwilling to surrender its hard-won freedoms. These voices of resistance not only challenged the government's actions but also served as a reminder of the power of ordinary people in shaping the course of history.

Chapter Six; The Lifting of Martial Law

Parliamentary Actions Against Martial Law

The National Assembly's swift response to President Yoon Suk Yeol's declaration of martial law marked a turning point in the unfolding crisis. Opposition lawmakers, who held a majority in the assembly, condemned the move as a blatant overreach of executive power and a violation of the constitution. Within hours of the declaration, they convened an emergency session to counteract what they described as a "descent into authoritarianism."

During the heated session, impassioned speeches echoed throughout the chamber. Lawmakers accused Yoon of undermining South Korea's democratic foundations and jeopardizing the nation's international reputation. "This is not governance; this is tyranny," one opposition leader declared, drawing applause from fellow members.

A motion to repeal martial law was introduced and passed with overwhelming support, showcasing a rare moment of unity among political factions typically divided by ideological differences. The resolution not only demanded the immediate cessation of martial law but also called for a full investigation into the circumstances that led to its declaration.

President Yoon's Decision to Rescind the Declaration

Facing mounting pressure from both the National Assembly and a furious public, President Yoon was forced to reconsider his position. The vote to lift martial law, while legally binding, was also a symbolic blow to his authority. It underscored his dwindling support, not only among lawmakers but also within his own administration.

In a nationally televised address, Yoon announced the rescission of martial law, citing a desire to "restore unity and stability." However, his tone was defiant. He defended his initial decision as necessary to safeguard the nation against what he called "imminent threats from internal and external forces."

The president's address did little to quell public outrage. Critics argued that his reversal was not an act of reconciliation but a reluctant concession to political and social pressure. "He didn't admit fault or offer an apology," noted a political analyst on a popular news program. "This was damage control, not accountability."

The immediate lifting of martial law brought a sense of relief to a nation under duress. Soldiers were ordered to withdraw from public spaces, curfews were lifted, and media restrictions were eased. However, the scars left by the declaration lingered, leaving many South Koreans questioning the stability of their democracy.

Implications of the Lifting for Governance

The rescission of martial law raised pressing questions about the state of governance in South Korea. The crisis had exposed significant cracks in the nation's political framework, particularly the relationship between the executive branch and other arms of government.

One of the most glaring issues was the unchecked authority of the presidency. While South Korea's democratic system includes mechanisms to balance power, Yoon's ability to declare martial law without prior consultation highlighted the potential for executive overreach. This sparked widespread calls for constitutional reforms to prevent similar crises in the future.

The military's role during the crisis also came under scrutiny. Many citizens and lawmakers expressed concern over the willingness of military leaders to comply with the president's orders, even when those orders appeared to contravene democratic principles. Proposals to strengthen civilian oversight of the armed forces gained traction in the aftermath of the crisis. For opposition parties, the lifting of martial law was both a victory and a challenge. While they had succeeded in curbing the president's authority, the road ahead required careful navigation. Calls for impeachment were growing louder, and public expectations for accountability were high. At the same time, the opposition faced the delicate task of addressing the grievances of those who had supported martial law, including conservative factions concerned about national security.

For the average citizen, the lifting of martial law brought a mix of relief and lingering apprehension. Streets that had been eerily quiet under military patrols once again buzzed with life. Shops reopened, protests resumed, and families gathered to discuss the events of the past days. "I feel like I can breathe again," said a small business owner in Incheon. "But the fear isn't gone. What's stopping this from happening again?"

The return to normalcy was bittersweet for many, especially those who had endured arrests, injuries, or other hardships during the crisis. Human rights organizations reported cases of individuals detained during martial law who were still awaiting legal recourse. Advocacy groups called for immediate action to address these injustices, emphasizing the importance of holding the government accountable. Behind the political maneuvers and legislative victories lay the human cost of the martial law declaration. Families mourn loved ones injured or lost during protests, while others grapple with the emotional toll of living under constant surveillance.

One poignant story was that of a teacher in Seoul who, during martial law, had organized secret gatherings to educate her students about their constitutional rights. When asked how she felt about the lifting of martial law, she said, "I'm relieved, but I'm also angry. We shouldn't have to fight for freedoms that are supposed to be guaranteed."

Such sentiments were echoed across the country. For many South Koreans, the crisis served as a wake-up call about the fragility of democracy. It inspired renewed civic engagement, with citizens pledging to remain vigilant in the face of potential future threats to their freedoms. The lifting of martial law marked the end of an extraordinary chapter in South Korea's history, but its implications would resonate for years to come. While the immediate crisis had been resolved, it left behind a nation grappling with questions about leadership, accountability, and the resilience of its democratic institutions.

The collective relief was tempered by a deep understanding of the work that lay ahead. For South Koreans, the crisis was a stark reminder of the importance of protecting democratic values—a challenge they appeared more than ready to embrace.

Chapter Seven; Impeachment Proceedings

Grounds for Impeachment: Legal Framework

The impeachment proceedings against President Yoon Suk Yeol began in the wake of his controversial declaration of martial law. Opposition lawmakers, buoyed by public outcry and their parliamentary majority, initiated the process under Article 65 of South Korea's Constitution, which allows for the removal of a president who has violated the law or the Constitution.

The legal arguments for impeachment were straightforward. Critics argued that Yoon's declaration of martial law lacked both justification and adherence to the constitutional guidelines that govern such actions. Under South Korea's Constitution, martial law can only be declared in cases of severe threats to national security, such as war or large-scale insurrection. Yoon's rationale—accusing opposition lawmakers of colluding with North Korea—was deemed speculative and unsupported by evidence.

Furthermore, the imposition of martial law violated several constitutional provisions, including those protecting civil liberties, freedom of assembly, and press freedom. Legal experts pointed to these violations as clear grounds for impeachment, emphasizing that the president had not only overstepped his authority but also undermined the democratic foundations of the nation.

Political Maneuvering and Party Dynamics

The road to impeachment was far from straightforward. While opposition parties held a two-thirds majority in the National Assembly—a requirement for passing the motion—achieving unity among lawmakers was a delicate task.

The Democratic Party, which spearheaded the impeachment effort, faced pressure to maintain cohesion within its ranks. Any sign of division could weaken the momentum of the proceedings. Behind closed doors, party leaders worked tirelessly to align their members, addressing concerns and rallying support for the motion.

Smaller opposition parties, initially hesitant to commit, eventually joined the effort after intense negotiations. Their support was secured through promises of future collaboration on shared policy goals, as well as assurances that the impeachment would be conducted fairly and transparently.

The ruling People Power Party (PPP), meanwhile, scrambled to defend the president. Party leaders launched a counter-narrative, portraying the impeachment as a politically motivated attack rather than a legitimate response to constitutional violations. Some lawmakers within the PPP, however, expressed private concerns about Yoon's actions, leading to rumors of potential defections. As the impeachment motion gained traction, the political atmosphere grew increasingly charged. Lawmakers on both sides of the aisle engaged in heated debates, with some accusing each other of betrayal and opportunism. Public opinion polls revealed deep divisions among citizens, reflecting the polarized nature of the political landscape.

The Vote and Immediate Consequences

The day of the impeachment vote was marked by tension and anticipation. Crowds gathered outside the National Assembly building, holding banners and chanting slogans for and against the motion. Security was heightened to prevent clashes between opposing groups.

Inside the assembly chamber, the atmosphere was no less charged. Lawmakers delivered impassioned speeches, some pleading for justice and accountability, others warning of the dangers of political instability. As the roll call began, the nation held its breath. When the final vote count was announced, the motion to impeach President Yoon Suk Yeol had passed with a significant majority. The decision sent shockwaves through South Korea, marking only the second time in the country's history that a sitting president had been impeached. Under South Korea's legal framework, the impeachment vote immediately suspended Yoon's presidential powers. Prime Minister Han Duck-soo assumed the role of acting president, tasked with maintaining stability during the interim period. The Constitutional Court now had 180 days to deliberate and decide whether to uphold or overturn the impeachment.

The impeachment vote drew mixed reactions from the public. For many, it was a moment of triumph—a victory for democracy and a testament to the power of collective action. Citizens who had participated in protests against martial law celebrated the decision, viewing it as validation of their efforts. "I feel like we've taken a step toward justice," said a young activist in Seoul. "But this is just the beginning. We need to stay vigilant."

Others, particularly supporters of President Yoon, saw the impeachment as a betrayal of the democratic process. They accused opposition lawmakers of exploiting the crisis for political gain and warned that the decision could lead to further instability. The international community closely monitored the developments, with foreign governments and organizations offering varied responses. While some praised South Korea for upholding democratic accountability, others expressed concern about the potential impact on the country's governance and its ability to address pressing issues, such as tensions with North Korea.

The impeachment of President Yoon left South Korea at a crossroads. The suspension of his powers created a power vacuum that the acting president and the National Assembly had to navigate carefully. Ensuring political stability while addressing the deep divisions within the country became the top priority for the interim government.

The Constitutional Court's role in the process added another layer of complexity. The court's decision, expected within six months, would determine whether Yoon would be permanently removed from office or reinstated. Legal experts predicted a rigorous examination of the evidence, with the court balancing constitutional principles against the political realities of the situation. For opposition lawmakers, the impeachment vote was a hard-won victory, but it also came with significant responsibility. The public expected them to not only hold Yoon accountable but also address the systemic issues that had allowed the crisis to unfold. Proposals for constitutional reforms, including measures to limit presidential powers and enhance checks and balances, gained renewed attention.

The impeachment proceedings against President Yoon Suk Yeol represented a defining moment in South Korea's democratic journey. The events highlighted both the strengths and vulnerabilities of the nation's political system, demonstrating the resilience of its institutions while exposing the challenges that lay ahead.

As South Koreans grappled with the uncertainty of the future, one thing was clear: the fight to safeguard democracy was far from over. The next steps—both in the courtroom and in the political arena—would shape the nation's trajectory for years to come.

Chapter Eight; Comparative Analysis

Martial Law in Other Democracies

The declaration of martial law in South Korea under President Yoon Suk Yeol is not an isolated case; historically, several democracies have resorted to similar measures during times of national crisis. However, the application and consequences of martial law in these instances provide valuable lessons for South Korea as it navigates its own turbulent period.

In the United States, martial law has been declared only in rare and extreme circumstances, such as during the Civil War and the 1992 Los Angeles riots. In both cases, the federal government exercised military control over certain regions, although these measures were intended as temporary and primarily focused on restoring public order. While the American Constitution allows for such actions, it also includes robust mechanisms for oversight, making it difficult for any one branch of government to unilaterally impose martial law without significant scrutiny.

Similarly, in the Philippines, martial law has been declared several times, most notably by President Ferdinand Marcos in 1972, a move that led to nearly a decade of authoritarian rule. Marcos justified his declaration with claims of threats from communist insurgents, but the real impact was the erosion of democratic freedoms, as the military gained sweeping powers to suppress dissent. The aftermath of Marcos's martial law rule serves as a cautionary tale, illustrating the danger of executive overreach and the long-lasting damage to democratic institutions. South Korea, in its present situation, faces a crucial crossroads: will the martial law crisis result in strengthening democratic safeguards, or will it embolden a shift toward autocratic governance?

In Turkey, President Recep Tayyip Erdoğan faced significant political unrest in 2016, which led to an attempted coup against his government. Following the failed coup, Erdoğan declared a state of emergency, a less extreme form of martial law, but one that allowed the government to impose sweeping restrictions on civil liberties, arrest political opponents, and suppress media freedoms.

While the state of emergency was meant to restore order, it raised serious concerns about human rights violations and the consolidation of power in Erdoğan's hands. South Korea must tread carefully to avoid similar pitfalls, where the temporary suspension of rights could become permanent in the face of rising political instability.

Lessons Learned from Historical Precedents

The history of martial law in democracies reveals crucial lessons for South Korea, especially regarding the balance between national security and civil liberties. One of the most important takeaways is the need for clear legal frameworks and oversight mechanisms when declaring such extreme measures. In the cases of both the U.S. and the Philippines, martial law declarations were subject to legal challenges, and in many instances, these declarations were deemed unconstitutional or temporary. South Korea's legal system must ensure that any future emergency powers are used responsibly, with built-in checks to prevent abuse.

Another key lesson is the importance of transparency and accountability. In every instance where martial law was declared, there were calls for greater transparency in government actions. The lack of clarity surrounding the reasons for President Yoon's declaration of martial law has sparked widespread distrust among the South Korean public. Future leaders must be more forthcoming about the rationale behind such decisions, and the consequences of those decisions should be fully disclosed to the public in a timely manner. Without transparency, the risk of alienating citizens and eroding trust in democratic institutions is significant.

Moreover, historical cases emphasize the importance of maintaining a commitment to democratic values even in the face of crisis. In some instances, leaders who declared martial law were able to capitalize on the fear and instability to centralize power, undermining the democratic systems that allowed them to come to office in the first place. For South Korea, the challenge will be to manage political crises without compromising the rights and freedoms that are central to its democratic identity.

The response to President Yoon's martial law declaration will set the tone for how South Korea handles similar challenges in the future.

The Role of International Relations in Martial Law Declarations

International relations play a critical role in the declaration and the lifting of martial law. In a globalized world, no country exists in isolation, and the actions of one nation can have wide-reaching effects on its international standing. South Korea, with its tense relations with North Korea and its strategic importance in the region, is particularly vulnerable to the repercussions of its domestic decisions.

When President Yoon declared martial law, many foreign governments, particularly those in the West, expressed concern over the potential erosion of South Korea's democratic values. International organizations, including the United Nations and human rights groups, were quick to condemn the imposition of martial law, urging South Korea to adhere to its international obligations regarding the protection of human rights.

This external pressure played a significant role in forcing President Yoon to rescind the declaration within hours, as it was clear that the international community was watching closely.

For South Korea, navigating the delicate balance between domestic governance and international relations will continue to be a critical challenge. Martial law, especially in the context of rising tensions with North Korea, could be perceived as a sign of weakness, inviting external interference in South Korea's internal matters. Furthermore, any future imposition of martial law could jeopardize South Korea's standing with key allies and affect its position in international negotiations, particularly those related to security and trade.

The Global Impact of Martial Law

Martial law declarations in democracies often attract global attention, as they have the potential to reshape not only domestic politics but also international relations. In South Korea's case, the martial law crisis and its aftermath have been closely scrutinized by countries in the region, including Japan, China, and the United States.

Each of these nations has a vested interest in South Korea's stability, and any political instability within the country could ripple through the region, affecting everything from trade relations to security concerns.

For example, the lifting of martial law in South Korea prompted a cautious sigh of relief from many nations, but there is an underlying concern about the precedent it sets. Should similar situations arise in the future, the international community may have less faith in South Korea's ability to resolve such crises through democratic means. Thus, the global impact of South Korea's martial law declaration extends far beyond the immediate political consequences, affecting its ability to maintain strong alliances and navigate the complex geopolitical landscape of East Asia. The comparative analysis of martial law declarations in other democracies provides South Korea with a valuable perspective on its own political crisis. While the country faces unique challenges, the lessons learned from past instances of martial law can inform the way forward. South Korea's response to this crisis will not only shape its future domestic governance but also influence its position on the world stage.

The international community will be watching closely, and South Korea's ability to restore political stability without sacrificing democratic principles will be its most significant challenge.

Chapter Nine; Future Implications for South Korea

Political Stability and Governance Challenges

The unfolding political crisis surrounding President Yoon Suk Yeol's declaration of martial law and subsequent impeachment proceedings leaves South Korea facing a crucial test for its political stability. The immediate consequences of the martial law incident have already rippled through the country's political landscape, but the longer-term effects will determine whether South Korea emerges from this period more resilient or more fractured.

As the dust settles, South Korea finds itself at a crossroads, with the need to balance the demands for political reform and stability. The temporary suspension of presidential powers and the ascension of Prime Minister Han Duck-soo as acting president highlight the fragility of governance in a nation deeply divided by partisan politics.

In the wake of Yoon's impeachment, there is a growing consensus that the current political system may be too prone to manipulation, especially when the executive branch faces severe challenges from a polarized legislature. The events surrounding the martial law declaration have underscored the limitations of South Korea's democratic institutions, particularly the vulnerability of its checks and balances system when confronted with an assertive, embattled president.

This situation brings into focus the need for reforms that can restore faith in the country's political structures. Many experts and political analysts now argue that South Korea must strengthen its mechanisms for holding public officials accountable while preserving political stability. For instance, reforms could include limiting the president's emergency powers, ensuring greater transparency in political decision-making, and establishing clearer legal frameworks for times of crisis. However, achieving these reforms would require consensus across South Korea's fragmented political parties, which, given the current climate of distrust and division, may prove to be a significant hurdle.

Another critical aspect of political stability is public confidence in the electoral process. South Koreans have witnessed firsthand the power struggles and political infighting that have defined recent months, and many feel disillusioned by the seeming inability of their leaders to prioritize the country's well-being over personal and partisan interests. For the country to regain its stability, rebuilding this trust in both the government and the political system is essential. Political leaders will have to demonstrate a genuine commitment to serving the people and upholding democratic principles above political gains.

The Role of International Relations, Especially with North Korea

South Korea's international relations, especially with its neighbor to the north, will be a significant factor in the aftermath of the martial law crisis. North Korea has long been a source of tension in the region, and any political instability within South Korea presents an opportunity for the North to capitalize on the situation.

In recent years, North Korea has actively sought to test South Korea's resilience and challenge the international community's resolve in maintaining pressure on the regime. With South Korea's political situation in flux, North Korea may perceive this as an opening to advance its own agenda, whether through provocations or diplomatic pressure. In this delicate environment, maintaining a unified front with key international allies, particularly the United States, is crucial.

However, the political crisis within South Korea could also present opportunities for new diplomacy and engagement with North Korea. While South Korea's leadership remains mired in internal turmoil, the need for stability and regional cooperation will likely encourage fresh efforts to rebuild relations with Pyongyang. Whether this leads to a breakthrough or another breakdown in talks remains uncertain. What is clear, however, is that any significant shifts in South Korea's domestic politics could directly impact its approach to North Korea and its role in the broader East Asian geopolitical landscape.

As the country's political crisis unfolds, its foreign policy direction, particularly in relation to North Korea, may become more unpredictable. South Korea will need to work closely with its allies to navigate these complexities, ensuring that its internal issues do not compromise its strategic interests on the global stage.

Prospects for Democratic Resilience

The martial law crisis and impeachment proceedings in South Korea have tested the nation's democratic resilience, but they have also created an opportunity for reflection and reform. South Korea's democratic system, though young by global standards, has made significant strides since the end of military rule in the late 1980s. The impeachment of former President Park Geun-hye in 2017 demonstrated the country's commitment to holding leaders accountable, even at the highest levels.

Now, South Koreans face another crossroads, and the question remains: will their democracy emerge stronger, or will the crisis lead to further erosion of public trust in their institutions? The key to democratic resilience lies in how the political system adapts to new challenges and maintains its foundational values.

One potential avenue for strengthening South Korea's democracy lies in electoral reform. The current political system, with its hyper partisan nature and dominance of a few major political parties, often leads to deadlock and makes meaningful cooperation difficult. Introducing proportional representation or other electoral changes could give rise to new political voices, diminishing the power of entrenched elites and fostering greater diversity in political discourse. Furthermore, the role of civil society in strengthening democracy cannot be overstated. The South Korean public has been an active participant in the nation's democratic processes, from the candlelight protests that ousted Park Geun-hye to the widespread opposition to martial law. These mobilizations signal that South Koreans are deeply invested in the future of their country's democracy.

As such, it is crucial that the government recognizes and supports these efforts, ensuring that citizens remain engaged in the political process and that their voices are heard. The media, too, plays a pivotal role in ensuring democratic accountability. In recent years, South Korean media outlets have grown increasingly diverse and critical of the government, playing a vital role in holding officials accountable. However, there are growing concerns about media consolidation and the potential for political pressure on journalists. A thriving, independent media landscape is a cornerstone of democracy, and any attempts to undermine press freedom would only serve to weaken the democratic fabric of South Korean society.

The events surrounding President Yoon's declaration of martial law and the subsequent impeachment proceedings have placed South Korea's democracy under intense scrutiny. As the nation moves forward, the ability to learn from this crisis and adapt will determine whether South Korea emerges stronger or more vulnerable. Political stability, international relations, and democratic resilience will all be key to shaping the nation's future.

The road ahead is uncertain, but South Korea's history shows that it has the strength to overcome its challenges and continue its journey as a vibrant democracy.

Conclusion

The events surrounding President Yoon Suk Yeol's declaration of martial law, followed by the intense political fallout and impeachment proceedings, have undeniably marked a pivotal moment in South Korea's modern history. These unprecedented actions have not only tested the resilience of the country's democratic institutions but have also highlighted the deeply entrenched divisions within its political landscape. However, this crisis, while disruptive, also presents a critical opportunity for South Korea to reflect, reassess, and reinforce its commitment to democratic values and political stability.

At the heart of this situation is the tension between maintaining national security and safeguarding individual freedoms. President Yoon's martial law declaration, though short-lived, raised significant questions about the balance of power in South Korea's government. In times of crisis, leaders often seek to wield extraordinary powers to restore order and protect the nation, but such powers come with inherent risks.

The public's swift rejection of martial law and the subsequent impeachment push suggest that South Koreans are not willing to trade their hard-earned democratic freedoms for short-term stability. This strong commitment to democracy is a positive sign that, despite the political chaos, the country's democratic foundations remain intact and robust.

However, the political instability that followed the martial law declaration underscores the fragility of South Korea's current political system. The ideological rift between the ruling party and opposition factions, as well as the sharp partisan divides that characterized much of the debate surrounding Yoon's leadership, point to a need for reform. There is a growing consensus that South Korea's political system may benefit from adjustments that can reduce polarization and enhance cooperation among lawmakers. This is essential for ensuring the long-term stability of the nation, especially as the political climate becomes more unpredictable. Reforms could include changes to the electoral system, improvements in the transparency of governance, and the establishment of stronger checks and balances that protect against executive overreach.

The martial law crisis also brought into sharp focus South Korea's role on the global stage. Its international allies, particularly the United States, were watching closely as events unfolded. South Korea's standing in the international community could have been severely damaged had martial law been allowed to stand. Fortunately, the swift action by the National Assembly to lift the declaration, combined with international pressure, prevented a greater crisis.

Yet, the situation demonstrates how domestic instability can have global ramifications, particularly in a region as geopolitically charged as East Asia. South Korea must continue to navigate its complex relationship with North Korea and other regional players while maintaining its democratic integrity. Despite the challenges, South Korea's democratic system has proven to be resilient. The country's commitment to the rule of law, as demonstrated by the impeachment process, reflects the strength of its democratic institutions. South Korea has faced crises in the past, such as the 2017 impeachment of President Park Geun-hye, and emerged stronger as a result.

The current crisis, while daunting, can serve as another test that will ultimately lead to the strengthening of South Korea's democratic practices, provided that the lessons of this moment are learned and acted upon.

Looking forward, the future of South Korea's democracy hinges on the country's ability to adapt to its changing political landscape. The people of South Korea have shown that they are willing to stand up for their democratic rights, and this engagement will be key to safeguarding the country's future. The next steps for the nation involve not only ensuring that the current crisis is resolved in a way that preserves democratic norms but also looking ahead to implement structural reforms that can mitigate future risks. Strengthening public institutions, enhancing the political culture of cooperation, and fostering an informed, active citizenry will be essential for overcoming the current crisis and ensuring that South Korea remains a stable and vibrant democracy.

In conclusion, the events surrounding President Yoon's martial law declaration are far from the end of South Korea's democratic journey. They represent a challenge, but also an opportunity for growth and reflection. South Korea's political resilience, driven by its commitment to democracy, the rule of law, and civil liberties, will ultimately shape its future. The path ahead is not without its challenges, but South Korea has the strength, experience, and determination to navigate them. As the nation moves forward, it must embrace the lessons learned from this crisis to build a more inclusive, transparent, and stable political system that can weather future storms and continue to thrive on the global stage.

www.ingramcontent.com/pod-product-compliance
Lightning Source LLC
Chambersburg PA
CBHW071108240526
45469CB00006BD/2380